two peas

Sister to Sister

Serena

Compton

For Peggy, from Poughkeepsie and beyond, my forever friend. . . .
—L. C.-R.

For Romare Bearden, James Kerry Marshall, Leonardo Drew, Henry O. Tanner,
and all of the other African-American artists who have inspired me.
—J. E. R.

"We changed the whole game."
—Serena Williams

SIMON & SCHUSTER BOOKS FOR YOUNG READERS
An imprint of Simon & Schuster Children's Publishing Division
1230 Avenue of the Americas, New York, New York 10020
Text copyright © 2018 by Lesa Cline-Ransome
Illustrations copyright © 2018 by James E. Ransome
All rights reserved, including the right of reproduction in whole or in part in any form.
SIMON & SCHUSTER BOOKS FOR YOUNG READERS is a trademark of Simon & Schuster, Inc.
For information about special discounts for bulk purchases,
please contact Simon & Schuster Special Sales at 1-866-506-1949 or business@simonandschuster.com.
The Simon & Schuster Speakers Bureau can bring authors to your live event.
For more information or to book an event, contact the Simon & Schuster Speakers Bureau
at 1-866-248-3049 or visit our website at www.simonspeakers.com.
Book design by Laurent Linn
The text for this book was set in Chaparral Pro.
The illustrations for this book were rendered in cut paper, pencil, and acrylic paints.
Manufactured in China
0519 SCP
10 9 8 7 6 5
CIP data for this book is available from the Library of Congress.
ISBN 978-1-4814-7684-3
ISBN 978-1-4814-7685-0 (eBook)

GAME CHANGERS

The Story of *Venus* and *Serena Williams*

WRITTEN BY
Lesa Cline-Ransome

ILLUSTRATED BY **James E. Ransome**

A Paula Wiseman Book
SIMON & SCHUSTER BOOKS FOR YOUNG READERS
New York London Toronto Sydney New Delhi

Venus and Serena Williams, V and Meeka, two peas in a pod, best friends. Everybody who saw them knew they were as close as two sisters could be.

They grew up in the shadows of each other. First Venus was born in June of 1980. Little sister Serena came right behind her in September of 1981. Whatever Venus did, Serena followed. So when their father took Venus to the tennis court to begin lessons, Serena begged to go along.

Six days a week they rose before the sun. Sleepy-eyed, the girls rolled out of the bed they shared, climbed into their dad's run-down VW bus, and squeezed between their three older sisters, racquets, and a shopping cart filled with tennis balls and brooms. Between the early morning dark and the first light of the day, the girls stretched and warmed up, then swept the courts clean of broken glass and trash before their first practice of the day began.

Neighborhood folks laughed at a father, Richard, with tennis ambitions and a Compton address, but Richard's dreams soared far beyond the rough-and-tumble streets outside of Los Angeles County, California.

From the beginning, tennis was a family affair. First with the three oldest sisters, Yetunde, Lyndrea, and Isha. When they lost interest, the younger girls stepped in. Richard practiced with Venus on one court while Oracene, their mother, hit with Serena on the other to the cheers of their sisters on the sidelines.

It wasn't long before their father's dreams became their own. Venus and Serena didn't have time for friends or sleepovers or trips to the mall. Tennis filled their days. Side by side, they whispered into the night. "Do you really think I can do it?" they'd ask each other. "Do you really think I have a chance?"

Sound asleep, tennis filled their dreams.

"If I didn't play tennis, I don't know where I'd be," Venus told everyone.

They threw footballs to improve their serves. Tossed racquets into the air to build strength. And chased secondhand tennis balls so flat they learned to run faster to hit their low bounce. Not having expensive training equipment and professional coaches meant they had to make up their own drills.

Off the courts they worked to improve their speed with track and their flexibility with ballet.

When gunshots rang out in the distance, Richard reminded them, "Never mind the noise. Just play."

But when shots from the neighborhood's rival gangs whizzed near the courts, the girls quickly learned to drop their racquets and lie still until the shooting stopped.

The public courts of East Compton Park, with grass poking through cracks in the cement and chain-link nets, looked nothing like the courts they saw on television where their favorites, John McEnroe, Monica Seles, and Pete Sampras, played.

By the time Venus was four she could hit five hundred tennis balls at every practice. By the time she was seven she began playing in junior tournaments. Playing on Compton's public courts kept the girls hidden from much of the tennis circuit, but when Venus won every single one of her sixty-three junior tournaments by age ten, with Serena not far behind, word of the Williams sisters spread. "Whatever you become, you become in your head first," their mother preached daily.

With their talent grew confidence. At twelve, Venus announced she would win Wimbledon.

In 1994, at fourteen years old, Venus played her first professional match at the Bank of the West Classic in California. Tennis critics took notice after the young newcomer's combination shots and her return of serve helped her soar past higher ranking players to advance to the second round. Overnight Venus went from an unclassified ranking to number three hundred thirteen in the world.

"Your time will come," Venus comforted Serena, sad to not be sharing the spotlight with her sister.

When the press surrounded Richard, asking if Venus would be the next number-one player, Richard smiled. "Have you seen my other daughter Serena play?"

One year later, it was Serena's turn. Within three short years, both girls ranked in the top fifty. Long-legged, brown-skinned, beaded cornrowed sisters stood out in a sea of white tennis attire, white fans, and white opponents. They dressed as they pleased in their own designs. During matches they hit so hard, sometimes the rubber bands in their hair broke, scattering beads across the court. Tennis had never seen anything quite like them.

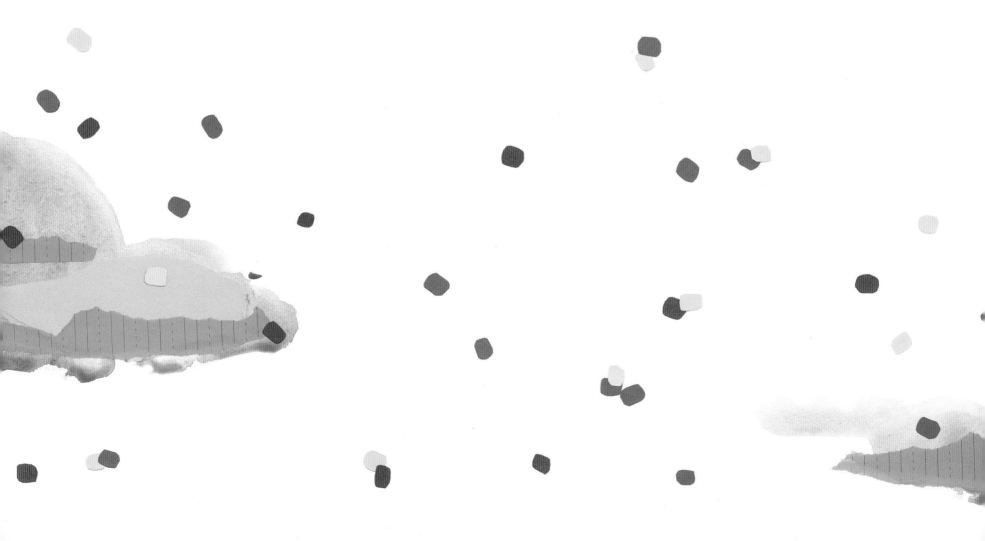

Many tennis fans cheered the energy and powerful playing of two fresh faces in tennis. But sometimes the sisters were threatened, booed, and taunted by others not happy to see them competing in a nearly all-white sport. They'd heard those words years earlier when their father brought in busloads of neighborhood kids to surround the practice courts as they played.

"Do your best," he told the kids, and paid each and every one to hurl the worst words his daughters might hear during their matches. Now, whenever those same words tumbled from the stands, they fell as flat as secondhand tennis balls. Words and gunshots, hatred and doubt couldn't slow the rise of the two sisters who called themselves "the greatest story in tennis."

They loved the same bands, laughed at the same jokes, wore the same clothes. Only on the court were they different. There Serena was as strong as Venus was fast. Venus was as gracious as Serena was aggressive.

Venus's long legs could carry her crosscourt in a couple of strides. At one hundred thirty miles per hour, her serve broke a world record. Serena chased down every ball, drilling them back to her opponents with high-powered ground strokes.

"I hate losing more than I love winning," Serena told reporters.

Life on the professional circuit meant traveling to tournaments and trekking as a family across the world to the Australian Open, French Open, Wimbledon in England, and New York City's U.S. Open to compete in one Grand Slam event after the next.

Not wanting to be separated during tournaments, the sisters shared hotel rooms. But the crowds loved it when they shared a court. *Sister Act, Smash Sisters, Sister Sister, Sister Slam* headlines screamed. Tickets were hard to come by on the days Venus and Serena were scheduled to play each other.

In doubles, knowing each other as well as they did paid off with win after win. But on opposite sides of the court, they were competitors first, sisters second.

At the Australian Open in 1998 Venus and Serena cheered each other as they both advanced. But each win also brought them closer to playing against each other. When they both advanced to the third round, they stood on opposite sides of the court for the very first time.

Venus was focused, but Serena, at sixteen years old, in her first major tournament, was shaky.

The match started slowly, each cautiously watching the game unfold against the opponent who knew her best. In their first set, Venus edged ahead after a tie-break. Serena looked to the players' box where her family sat, quiet for the first time. In the next set Venus took control.

Heads turned from left to right, right to left for a Venus victory, 7–6 and 6–1.

Serena was as sad for her loss as she was happy for Venus's win.

But then Venus kept winning, match after match, year after year, in each of their matchups.

"She knows how to beat me and knows my weaknesses better than anyone,"

Serena said of her big sister.

In 2000 they traveled to Sydney, Australia, for the Olympics and returned home wearing the gold medals they earned together for the United States in doubles.

In 2002 they faced each other again in the finals of the French Open. With each round she advanced, Serena pushed aside thoughts of their earlier matches and of Venus's successes.

While their family again sat quietly in the stands, Venus served big for the first set and took the lead, but Serena broke serve and won. The second set was hard fought, and the sisters rallied with down-the-line combinations, skidding from sideline to baseline until the final match point, when Venus cracked the ball into the net and the moment belonged to Serena. In two sets of 7–5 and 6–3, a victorious Serena stepped out of the shadow of her sister.

Venus ran off the court as the curious eyes of the crowd followed her. High into the stands Venus sprinted, snatched up her bag, and pulled out a camera.

"Nothing can keep me from celebrating when my best friend wins a match," Venus said proudly.

The crowd stood to applaud and Venus snapped shot after shot of Serena on the victory stand. Ranked numbers one and two in the world, Venus now followed Serena. Meeka and V, two peas in a pod, best friends and sisters celebrated being numbers one and two in life and in tennis.

• AFTERWORD •

After their Australian Open match in 2002, Venus and Serena became the first two sisters in tennis history to rank numbers one and two in the world.

They went on to meet in head-to-head matches more than twenty-five times—eight of those in Grand Slam finals.

Their numerous title wins include U.S. Open doubles and singles, Australian Open, French Open, and they have earned a combined total of eleven Wimbledon titles. Both won Olympic gold medals in 2000, 2008, and 2012. Venus was the first black woman to win Wimbledon since the legendary Althea Gibson in 1957. Serena was the first to win the U.S. Open since Althea in 1958.

"I am grateful to Althea Gibson for having the strength and courage to break through the racial barriers in tennis. Althea Gibson was the first African-American woman to rank number one and win Wimbledon, and I am honored to have followed in such great footsteps," Venus said.

Former tennis champion Chris Evert called Venus and Serena, "A phenomenon that once every hundred years comes around."

John McEnroe called Serena "The greatest player, I think, that ever lived."

Their success on and off the courts have made them two of the most popular athletes in history. Venus received a record-breaking contract with Reebok, the most ever offered for a female athlete. The sisters purchased shares of the Miami Dolphins football team in 2009 and became the first African-American women to own part of an NFL team.

Despite their many successes, health and personal setbacks followed them. In 2002 their parents, Richard and Oracene, divorced. In 2003 their oldest sister, Yetunde, was killed in a random act of gang violence in their Compton neighborhood. Serena had knee surgery and later suffered a pulmonary embolism. Then Venus was diagnosed with Sjogren's syndrome, an autoimmune disease, and both were required to take time off from tennis. Throughout these setbacks, the sisters have emerged stronger than ever, returning to win more titles. At thirty-five years old, Serena is the oldest number-one ranked player in World Tennis Association history.

During their rise through the tennis ranks, they continued their education and earned college degrees. Years later, after witnessing the health struggles Venus suffered, Serena began a pre-med track at the University of Massachusetts.

Activism off the court plays prominently in their lives. After a racially charged incident at the Indian Wells Master's Tournament in 2001, both sisters boycotted the tournament at great financial expense and lost rankings as a result.

Frustrated by the inequity in prize money awarded to male and female tennis players, in 2006 Venus wrote an editorial in *The Times of London* newspaper calling on Wimbledon to change its policy. "The message I like to convey to women and girls across the globe is that there is no glass ceiling. My fear is that Wimbledon is loudly and clearly sending the opposite message," she wrote. The following year, in 2007, Venus was the first woman to receive the same prize money as her male counterpart, Roger Federer, when she became the women's singles winner at Wimbledon.

During a goodwill trip to several African countries in 2006, Serena met with then President Abdoulaye Wade of Senegal and offered to build schools. In 2008 and 2010, Serena Williams Secondary Schools were built, providing a free education for all students. In 2011 she became a UNICEF International Goodwill Ambassador for her efforts to promote literacy and education throughout the world.

Venus and Serena live just miles apart in Florida.

• SOURCE NOTES •

"We changed the whole game." Diane Bailey, *Sports Families: Venus and Serena Williams* (New York: Rosen Central, 2010).

"Do you really . . . have a chance?" Serena Williams and Daniel Paisner, *On the Line* (New York: Grand Central Publishing, 2009).

"If I didn't play . . . where I'd be." Tim Adams, "What planet is she on?," *The Observer* (June 9, 2002).

"Never mind the noise . . . play." Richard Williams with Bart Davis, *Black and White: The Way I See It* (New York: Simon & Schuster, 2014).

"Whatever you become . . . your head first." Williams and Paisner, *On the Line*.

"Your time will come." Williams and Paisner, *On the Line*.

"Have you seen . . . daughter play?" Dave Rineberg, *Venus and Serena: My Seven Years as a Hitting Coach for the Williams Sisters* (Hollywood, Florida: Frederick Fell Publishers, 2002).

"Do your best." Williams with Davis, *Black and White*.

"the greatest . . . tennis." Steve Keating, "Williams sisters add new chapter to greatest story in tennis," *Reuters* (September 9, 2015).

"I hate losing . . . winning." *Venus and Serena*, directed by Maiken Baird and Michelle Major (New York: Magnolia Home Entertainment, 2013), DVD.

"She knows how . . . better than anyone." Sally Jenkins, "Venus and Serena: They're all grown up and still got each other's back," *Washington Post* (September 8, 2015).

"Nothing can keep . . . wins a match." Venus and Serena Williams with Hillary Beard, *Venus & Serena: Serving from the Hip* (Boston: Houghton Mifflin, 2005).

"I am grateful . . . in such great footsteps." Richard Lapchick, "Althea Gibson Must be Smiling over Venus, Serena," ESPN.com (July 9, 2008)

"A phenomenon . . . comes around." Claudia Rankine, "Her Excellence: What Serena Williams Means to Us," *New York Times* (December 21, 2015)

"The greatest . . . ever lived." Claudia Rankine, "Her Excellence: What Serena Williams Means to Us," *New York Times* (December 21, 2015)

• SELECTED BIBLIOGRAPHY •

Price, S.I. "Serena Williams: Sportsperson of the Year." *Sports Illustrated*, December 21, 2015: 66–86.

Rankine, Claudia. "Her Excellence: What Serena Williams Means to Us." *New York Times*, December 21, 2015.

Rineberg, Dave. *Venus and Serena: My Seven Years as a Hitting Coach for the Williams Sisters*. Hollywood, Florida: Frederick Fell Publishers, 2002.

Venus and Serena. DVD. Directed by Maiken Baird and Michelle Major. New York: Magnolia Home Entertainment, 2013.

Williams, Richard, with Bart Davis. *Black and White: The Way I See It*. New York: Simon & Schuster, 2014.

Williams, Serena, and Daniel Paisner. *On the Line*. New York: Grand Central Publishing, 2009.

Williams, Serena, and Venus Williams with Hillary Beard. *Venus and Serena: Serving from the Hip*. Boston: Houghton Mifflin, 2005.

• FURTHER READING •

Bailey, Diane. *Venus and Serena Williams: Tennis Champions*. New York: Rosen Central, 2010.

Cline-Ransome, Lesa. *Satchel Paige*. Illustrated by James E. Ransome. New York: Simon & Schuster Books for Young Readers, 2000.

Krull, Kathleen. *Wilma Unlimited: How Wilma Rudolph Became the World's Fastest Woman*. Illustrated by David Diaz. San Diego, California: Harcourt Brace, 1996.

Lang, Heather. *Queen of the Track: Alice Coachman, Olympic High-Jump Champion*. Illustrated by Floyd Cooper. Honesdale, Pennsylvania: Boyds Mills Press, 2012.

Vernick, Audrey. *She Loved Baseball: The Effa Manley Story*. Illustrated by Don Tate. New York: HarperCollins, 2010.

Venus and Serena

side by side

Sister to Sister